MW01120955

ESSENTIAL POETS SERIES 145

Canada Council Conseil des Arts
for the Arts du Canada

ONTARIO ARTS COUNCIL
CONSEIL DES ARTS DE L'ONTARIO

Guernica Editions Inc. acknowledges the support of
the Canada Council for the Arts.
Guernica Editions Inc. acknowledges the support of
the Ontario Arts Council.

MALCA LITOVITZ

FIRST DAY

GUERNICA
Toronto – Buffalo – Chicago – Lancaster (U.K.)
2008

Antonio D'Alfonso, editor
Guernica Editions Inc.
P.O. Box 117, Station P, Toronto (ON), Canada M5S 2S6
2250 Military Road, Tonawanda, N.Y. 14150-6000 U.S.A.

Distributors:
University of Toronto Press Distribution,
5201 Dufferin Street, Toronto (ON), Canada M3H 5T8
Gazelle Book Services, White Cross Mills, High Town,
Lancaster LA1 1XS U.K.
Independent Publishers Group,
814 N. Franklin Street, Chicago, Il. 60610 U.S.A.

First edition.
Printed in Canada.

Legal Deposit — First Quarter
National Library of Canada
Library of Congress Catalog Card Number: 2006923782
Library and Archives Canada Cataloguing in Publication
Litovitz, Malca Janice
First day / Malca Litovitz.— 1st ed.
(Essential poets series ; 145)
Poems.
ISBN-13: 978-1-55071-241-4
ISBN-10: 1-55071-241-1
I. Title. II. Series.
PS8573.I817F58 2006   C811'.54   C2006-901407-8

Contents

IN LOVING MEMORY

OF MY UNCLES,

IRVINE SHEINFIELD AND LOUIS SHENFELD

Image Angel

these wildflowers tell me
Nomi is close by

that patience and spring
happen when we aren't looking.

this plane overhead tells me
how vast the world is.

this wind blowing around me
caresses me like you do.

this bird singing in my tree
reminds me of the happiness here.

this woman scuttling by in her yellow hat
reminds me to survive.

this book, its pages fluttering,
holds a card which says you love me.

this truck rattling by speaks of accomplishments.
this black pen tells me who I am,

whispers of God's presence.

Morning Cat

The cat takes a few tenuous steps forward,
then retreats to her comfortable place
by the fence.

She hasn't decided what she wants to say yet.
She spends most of the morning
choosing the words.

She parts the stiff curtain of rules,
opening the windows wider still
in the yawn of morning.

Dundurn Castle

I sat on the edge of the lake
waiting to be lit from within;
peacocks in the children's zoo
furled their feathers –
turquoise like the walls in my mother's home.

On the parquet floor,
we danced to Monkee songs,
waved Bon Voyage streamers for Daisy.

She broke her heart
on her mother's butter knives and celery sticks,
heat waves and shattered mirrors
wrists could go through.
Floors splattered with blood
from children who ran too fast.

We covered the porch in iris leaves,
stashed Playboy centrefolds
in sewer hideouts,
Barbie's Dream House
crumpled and old.

Alice curls by the fire like her cat,
and the furniture moves in dreams.
The hall-light shines through a crack in the door
on the pages of Narnia
or a green copy of Anne of Avonlea
my mother read on prairie doorsteps –
grain elevators and gopher holes

rising rich in recall,
the smell of oranges on trains.
Memories lie pressed like old tulips.
Ride to Dundurn Castle on your bicycle
pigtails flying like Pippi Longstocking
off to see her cannibal king.

Climb Hamilton Mountain,
and look out over the city in slumber,
pink pollution clouds enveloping your day.
Your underwear will turn green
if you fall into that lake.

Downtown, the old Birk's clock
revolves in nineteenth-century curlicues.
Go to the White Grill –
have a Cherry Coke and Chicken-on-a-Bun.
See the Christmas lights
gleam all year round in Gore Park.
Jog on Kent Street, Aberdeen, Dundurn
as if we're all Scottish –
Earl Kitchener, Ryerson,
evergreen trees.

See this Canadian landscape:
steel mills and big chain fences.
The richest house gilded with plastic pineapples.

Men carry their black boxed lunches
wearing the scruffy dungarees and lumber jackets
my grandfather sold

while my grandmother sewed and made him lunch –
tea with lemon between the teeth.

Take the children to the park to swing at dusk –
let them see the parrots in the Dundurn Zoo.
Sit on the shore waiting for Sound and Light.

First Day

My kindergarten sits at the foot of the street,
brown ancd covered with ivy.

I'm dropped at the door
where I meet a girl named Susan.

Her hair is short and her nose pointed,
like Peter Pan's. I love and mistrust her immediately.

"Peter Pointer, Peter Pointer."
There is a song for each finger.

A sleepy child, I look off to a corner
as if a star were to appear there – elsewhere.

I hear the piano, see the teacher's fuzzy hair,
the towel for napping covered in faded roses.

Walking home early,
I mistake recess for the end of the day.

Poinsettia

I find no refreshment in the word, none in its rich red colour. It has meaning for someone else, a holiday I can't experience, wrapping paper I can't use, a tree in someone else's living room. I remember a small, wood-paneled room, gifts in wrapped packages scattered around the ground. Katy's mom cut the toast in neat rectangles to dunk in perfect soft-boiled eggs. Katy wore white go-go boots.

The poinsettia is barely a flower. It has no smell. It's a Hallmark card I can't read. Its points shut me out with their frozen shine and plastic aura.

The sky is pale navy, bordering on frail light above the black roofs and chimneys. Is that a small note of hope, a band of something lighter radiating from the housetops? At the front of the house, the trees are black shadows. No light has arrived, except for a winter blue sky. The trees crouch at the window, protective, combative. Growling slightly in their sleep, they are ready to spring into action if provoked.

November Tree

November tree,
grey cloud over,
the day settles windily down.

Lean for a moment,
slight song inside you

because you can't really sit
when the sun isn't out.
Thoughts may walk slowly,
but never stop.

You don't write poems with gloves on.

Wonderland

I remember reading Alice in bed while Mom and Dad had a bunch of houseguests over – they were chatting beneath the bright glow of the chandelier whose bulbs danced like strobe lights. Dad's laughter carried up over the stairs; Mom's hands in their pale pink manicured beauty served cookies on silver trays. All the while, they thought I was asleep with my door open a crack to let the light in just the way I liked it. My brother slept with the door tight shut. The hall light was on, high and humble, the none-too-clean little square fixture surrounded in wood. All this time, I kept the gooseneck lamp with its green shade on for as long as I could, and lay on my side reading my nice black copy of Alice. I gazed at the picture of her squashed into a house far too small for her, watching her grow and grow, all rumpled over on her side like that, taking on the very shape of the house. I watched her hair ripple down her back like sunlight on the path she followed with those two clunky knights in shining armour. I knew this was the story of my life – the vast, gleaming, funny adventure – and those knights would see me safely home, and I'd take care of them, too – we'd be sister and brother, mother and father to each other, and we'd giggle under the covers long after dark. Weary, I'd fall asleep. Maybe I still had the book open, Alice herself – dreaming, dreaming, like children do when they act naturally, one page after the other, breath by breath.

II

I am eight years old. Mom and Dad are having a party downstairs. Mom's made her macaroons and stuck them on a silver tray. Dad's going to have a drink and put a lampshade on his head, make Mrs. McGee laugh. Mom's coming up the stairs to tuck us in.

"Isaac, turn your light out."

"Martha, darling, it's very late. Put your book away now."

Mom comes over and tucks me in, gently pushes my hair from my forehead. She takes the book and puts it on my end table.

"Don't forget to take off your glasses, Martha."

I take off my pink harlequin glasses and lay them on the night table. Then I lie down.

As soon as Mom's gone, I turn the lamp back on and put on my glasses. I take out Alice like an illicit treasure. Reading is always somehow best when illicit, like a stolen kiss at midnight, like a candy kiss on Halloween that you think will break your teeth. I never liked Halloween kisses though. They weren't really a good toffee, and your teeth hurt forever. I preferred jawbreakers. You could suck them forever and take them out of your mouth to watch them change colours and shrink like Alice sometimes shrinks when she's bitten the small side of the cookie.

I get out of bed to go over to the mirror. I hold up a copy of *Through the Looking Glass* to see if the backwards language comes forward like Louis Carroll says it does. I wind a strand of hair around one finger, jab my thumb into my mouth although I know I mustn't, and curl comfortably into a little ball now. I turn the light out and soon am fast asleep.

Red Hydrant

For Liba Scheier, in memory

Liba, your father was a bully in a wheelchair.
Battered in Poland,
he battered you.
Sometimes, you are student,
your voice scratching the telephone lines,
but more, you are a female Odysseus,
making the long trek home.

Silvera, you picked coconuts from the side of the road,
saw shade trees and banana leaves at home,
ate guava in the morning.
Your mother offered everything with an open hand –
sliced oranges and made the bed
you could return to from anywhere in the world.

I thank God for my kind father,
his blue eyes benign.
The house I lived in had a red fire hydrant and Mother's lilacs.
Safe little Penates, household god,
beacon to the lack of emergencies.

Black Leather Jacket

For Michael Kleinberg, in memory

chic little piece
with worn-out sleeves
zipped-up jack kerouac

the man who wore you
was strangled
but you live on.

I used to think you had gone out of fashion.

I had to wait for the styles to change.

Snow Falls Quietly

snow falls quietly, the season changes

      spring arrives and disappears
like you on my doorstep,
      gifts quietly packaged in brown paper
pretending they aren't there

The Ceremony

Twenty-three years old. She has wavy brown hair parted at the side. She wears a camel-coloured cashmere sweater over a white brassiere that accentuates her breasts. She has a slim waist. She is wearing a long skirt that hugs her hips and descends gracefully, sturdy high-heeled leather shoes. She slips a silk trench coat over her shoulders, grabs a clutch bag from a table, and leaves her bungalow. The little china dog doorstopper looks loving. She heads over to the synagogue, where she has an appointment with the rabbi. They discuss her upcoming wedding. She crosses her legs in her sexy beige stockings and takes her harlequin glasses out of their brown case.

"The ceremony is the last day of January," she says.

The rabbi leans forward, his wire-framed glasses mirroring hers. She feels absurdly safe when he puts his arms around her shoulders. He rises and tugs gently at the Venetian blinds. He starts to caress her body. She can feel his fingertips on her breasts even though she is wearing the sweater and bra. He touches her legs, and his hands feel marvellous on the silky stockings. His fingers wander up to the top of her legs and creep over the top of her stockings.

"May I?" he asks as he undoes the little snap that keeps her stocking up.

She nods as he undoes the other snap and slowly slides her stocking down her shapely leg. He kisses her knee. He holds her foot in his hand.

Birthday

First ray of sun
calling me to a sun-dazzled year.

Look how God lights the sky
brighter than the curtains
and out the other window,
soft mauve.

Surely, good news is travelling swiftly
through the sleeping city; its dark houses
crouched in flannel positions.

A birthday hand
stretches its fingers of fortune,
palm lines extending gladly.

Let me enter this day in celebration,
expectation of happy shrieks of light
in a radiant sky.

I shall dress in red and black,
crimson joy,
lie down with my love
in wrapping paper –
cradle poems for his hands.

Blessings

She pronounces her benediction
on her pen, her dress,
her croissants and cheese.

Moroccan espresso cups
hold sugary strength
this morning.

She offers her blessings
to all who came before her
and to those who will follow,
and to that man she will write poems with
by a spring river.

The Current

Let us bless this flow of life which revives us,
sustains us, and brings us to this time.
Marcia Falk, "Sheheyanu,"
The Book of Blessings

Nightshade, pre-dawn –
and a garden lit
by a bald flash of sun
in a dusty sky.
Spring ice thaws:
the river flows again.

You write of the love
which sustains us,
its silent chord.

"Let us acknowledge the source of life,
source of all nourishment."

You feed me Casablanca tea.
We breathe in its fragrance –
cardamon, mint –
the singer from Afghanistan
pouring summer refreshment.

I am your alder grove
growing by the side of the road.

Forest Home

Yellow and white snapdragons
open their trumpet mouths.
Purple irises, some star-shaped,
petals closed, sexual.

We lie on the picnic table
gazing at a cantaloupe moon.
I tuck my head in your arms
thinking how happy we are with nothing.

The sky is our bedroom,
the stars our reading lamp,
moonlit tables for poetry.

You hold my hand for the climb
down creaky stairs of twigs and branches,
hang my coat on the nearest tree.

Day And Night

But his delight is in his Torah...
in his Torah, he meditates day and night.
And he shall be like a tree planted
by streams of water...

Psalm 1

You are here with me
in this solitary moment
at the sunlit table.

You are between every line,
as my writing hand
makes shadows on the fresh page.

We write the same renga,
our lines overlapping,
waves on the shore.

The moon misted over
when you read my poems
by a thin flashlight.

I lay on a picnic table gazing at the stars.
You lay down beside me after reading the verses
and held me close.

I offered you thin black panties
to smell in the dark forest,
and you held them to your face.

The black trunk of a tree in Cornell
holds the holiness of a thousand students
crossing the green quad

to an old stone façade,
a palace of learning
like the round table in heaven

where we can write like this
excavating the Word
from ancient texts.

Coyote

Don't let me be mad, let me pick up my paint instead.
I'll meet you in a dark corner of the garden,
there where the forest enters the park to make it sing.

I'll pray with you looking out at white water
that whistles through the deepest part of the sacred walk.
I'll touch you wet and let you brush my hair.

I need to find Coyote still, find him increasingly –
make him tremble in my kitchen –
make the walls of my house laugh.

Let's sit across the table from each other,
the words spilling into tea cups.

Lemon Kitchen

I brought you yellow flowers,
Amor,
to place in a green tea jar.
Music shelf tipped in birds,
a Mexican bus over the doorway,
a guitar hung on a wall.
In a garden of wildflowers and trees,
we suckle each other's poems,
content in this hour.
Dylan outdoes himself,
and the Tambourine Man
reappears.

Balancing Act

The rope dancer accompanies herself with her shadows.
Man Ray

She finds the light and shadows,
the magic wand of dance
waved like a child's pinwheel, fluttering.

Her ropes enter pools of light –
a little white castle illuminates her foreground.
She smiles to reassure herself in the mirror.

Her practiced legs perform for her,
black sleeves flicker in the darkest spaces.
The dance contains studies in black and white.

He loves me, he loves me not.
Herein lies all the difference.

Song for Miriam

Raise your timbrel and dance,
stand in the centre
of the jubilant women
and make this night
an exultation.

Bless your swim
in the well of happiness
which follows you into the desert,
into this prophetic land.

Lead us, Miriam,
into the dance.
The cool night extends her warm embrace,
wraps her shawl about you with loving hands.

Wizard Shop on Bloor

The connections between us
stretch their arms
like the strings on the clown,
his red hair and yellow bow-tie
pleasing you as you lift him down
from the ceiling and wrap him in tissue.

Receiver

I am the receiver
of the bounteous gifts of friends.
Here in my illness,
lunch at Milk 'n' Honey,
strolls in Elora's cedar forest,
cards by the bushel.
Small things, too:
notebooks shaped like ruby slippers
and ladybugs, dancers to remind me
of who I am.
Thumbnail red hat,
a Zen garden I can brush
from my hospital bed,
my feet dancing again.

Petrushka, 1949

After a painting by Franz Kline

The stylist finds the places holding desire and fear.
It's much more than a shampoo.
He finds the places in my skull that need release,
but only you speaking
the words I need to hear
can bring this deeper calm.

I am your Petrushka,
sad old clown to your Nijinsky –
your wild flight into dance.

Now, I lean my head
in my comical hat
trimmed like a tambourine.

My brow is creased.
I recline on whiteness,
an old woman
sinking into the softness around her face.

The Hearts

After a New Yorker cover, February 12, 2001

Ace of Hearts,
you wake up alone:
hand on pelvis,
fist of the warrior,
waiting.

Two of Hearts,
you hold your heart
in your hand,
a bag of candy
offered to the first passerby.
The bride is nowhere to be seen;
then, she eats your kiss,
a jujube,
throws you away.

Three of Hearts
on bended knees.
Romeo woos
in the garden of love,
while the bride's heart stands
on the precarious ledge,
leaning.

Four of Hearts,
the groom comes out
on the balcony and growls
for you to leave,

take your floral heart
with you.
The bride cranes on her long legs,
bending her head to you,
but not moving.

Five of Hearts,
smiles
holding the secret heart of love,
while the groom
furrows his brow,
stands on the edge
of the balcony.

You are happy now
on both knees,
the heart of your love
flowing above your head.

Six of Hearts,
an odd assortment –
you pirouette in the foyer,
and the angry groom
leaps down to grab your neck.

The bride hovers above you,
frightened for you both,
but secretly relishing
her hidden power.

Other lovers
stand and point at your ardour –
you hold your heart, a mirror.

Seven of Hearts:
a duel.
Your face almost feminine
next to the glowering, swirling brow
of the groom.
Your pistols are purple,
the guns of Israel –
they shoot
into the ether.
Five of us stand to watch you,
but your beloved is home
safe in bed.

Eight of Hearts:
an aria rises out of the heart of the groom you slew.
Despite your gentle demeanour,
you have knocked the man flat.
A gaggle of hearts surrounds you in your triumph.

Nine of Hearts,
the bride speaks:

At our wedding,
second husband of mine,
a chorus of red roses
sings in the upper pew
at Cambridge.
The priest wears his heart
on his head
and reads from Kahil Gibran.

Ten of Hearts –
an expanded circle.

The wife is pregnant with your eighth.
Your arms
do not reach around
her expanded waist.
They circle the globe,
various degrees of smiles
on the faces of your children.

The circular movements of heart:
the hips, the arms
in their natural rotation,
the way the seasons come and go
in the garden.

Low Nocturnal Moan

jazz riff in the morning –
   silk stockings in your voice mail,
our cries in the garden
   where the dog barks,
and the twigs crunch under our feet

daily prayer, daily rhythm –
   Spanish guitars before the moon sets –
out on a black October morning,
     singing

standing in the bus shelter
   on the corner
where the dark wind
   ruffles my hair –
tam pulled low –

every dark car approaching could be yours –

The Way You Talk

the woman in the park was playing with a small boy, the
white birds were gathering to eat from her hands the way
they do near St. Mark's Cathedral, the way they do on
mountain-tops when the bells are ringing, you have to sit
very still in a warm morning place the autumn leaves blow-
ing big orange clusters and large red vases full of fall
chrysanthemums, the robin sings in the garden, suddenly a
blue bird, while Lena Horne sings "Stormy Weather," in
the morning it's sweet, soon Ella Fitzgerald and you love
the jazz on your telephone, you love my message, you are
my spiritual husband and I like the way you talk.

Your Face

Your face in repose,
lined, strong, mature.
Your eyes send out sapphire sparks.

I paint your face with my eyes,
while yours are closed.

Your hand caresses my face,
    the small of my back.
We're sexual athletes, you say.
You think I lack inhibition,
but you made me this way.
Tapped open, I am radiant.

Your voice at midnight says my whole name.
I need to see you, to fill with light and air.
Your hands dance on my cheek, my body.

River Mapping

The Credit River is pumpkin; brown-hooded creatures dance on
    the shore.
The Ghengis is black, a giant in an old legend.
The Cam is full of the laughter of rippling puddles.
The Chinese River sings of hats and equanimity under a
    powerful sun.
Suzanne's river is orange; laundry flutters.
The kayak's river is a turbulent sword of light.
Om River is a storybook:
Poems open on our laps and a yellow picnic.
Judy's river ripples in rainbow ink.
Our water slickers gleam as the Moscow River unfolds itself,
a shawl by the banks of Grandmother's linen.
The river inside us is an ember in dark November.

River Gift

You point to a branch,
slow motion beauty,
freeze frame.

It bends down,
a tree crooking its elbow.

Thank you for the gift of thaw,
the black fork of flowing water
in the snowy river,
the gift of our eyes together.

The curtain covered in small flowers
blows in the sunlight;
we puff and bask
in each other's air.

Pas de deux

Barely a ripple in the noonday trees,
our hands linked, crossing the field,
we clamber down the brown slope.

Weeping guitars in our blood,
I feel you dancing in me now,
langorous and ineffable.

This softest, deepest dance
from behind, entering aslant.
Deep in body, wordless.

Night time is ours.
A dark table for our bed,
the moon's silver song.

Oneness

in my listening garden,
being is abundance –
    birds in the holy green –
we cling to each other,
      silent

Beauty Declared

My hand makes a shadow
on the page
like Peter Pan
looking for a stocking
in a Darling drawer.

Darling, starling –
sun rising now
in the glistening day –

a plane's rainbow sound
arcing over this garden,
beautiful because you said it was.

Beauty to Tears

Biblical currents of Sharon,
ancient language of the Songs.
Love-vow deepening
in the duet of dusk.
Onset of rain,
gentler than tears.

Strength, holiness descend
with the clouded sky.

Twilight is for lovers,
God said.
We are violet encroachment
of the night.

Beret

I
The gift

You were lying beside me; you rose to get your briefcase. I could see the photo in the top file, and a thrill shot through my body.

e.e. cummings is wearing a small black beret. There's a line between his eyebrows as though he's gazing very intently. His eyes are narrowed in order to see. His mouth is crooked, not smiling.

Coins of bright poetry gleam in the strong sun. I assimilate this with the photo of this brooding man, seeking truth in black and white.

My own beret wasn't lost on you. This gift: you understand the rich root of cummings in my imagination.

II
The dream

I met you in California. You were walking on the beach like Ferlinghetti. You were gazing at a starfish on the shore – bleached bones of beauty. You lay on the sand, brushed angels' wings.

"You're spread-eagled," I said.

You came and knelt behind me. You lifted my white shirt. I felt your warm hands on my back. I unbuttoned your soft trousers.

III
Advice

I must write with a hand on my breast. Naked. I don't need to be funny or pretty. I get up in the morning, beautiful in Bolivian cotton. I love you in your crinkled plaid pyjamas – the ones too small for you. You see the calm, flat plenitude of my gaze. You see the pain buried between brows and smooth that place with your fingers.

cummings' photo reminds me of you, whom I write about in rapid blue strokes.

Love Letters

You send me love letters
in postcards –
cummings –
his sharp black shoes.
Martha Graham caught in a Latinate embrace –
her illuminated face.

Here we stand in middle-aged contemplation –
my forehead suddenly serene,
my mouth unsmiling, real at last.
Your satisfaction calm
as I cover your hand.

I shall take care of you. "Someone to Watch over Me" –
plaintive until done upbeat.

Reading in Bed

How I long to read in bed with you, your voice on my pillow, white in my dreams, your poems on my nightstand, water for me to drink. Maple poems you read to me one auburn afternoon, one scarlet winter day. The river poured silver and the moon sat on my doorstep, a gift at dawn. I relax my tongue, stiffened by so much poetry and wine. My white robe is frayed, with soot-smeared cuffs the angel couldn't remove. These lines flow down the side of the lamp. I lay my head down on your thoughts, feel them coming to me through the pages of your book. You are reading Klima tonight, every gesture a gesture of love.

Self Talk

You are happy in this moment, reading a poem he wrote from the deepest side of him, and knowing you understand it. You are with him as he wades into the waters, the trombones wailing, the saxophones calling you home, the dolphins crying.

You cannot decide what to leave here and what to take home. Your belongings are heavy; they weigh you down.

They are unimportant. They are not who you are. You are this woman wrapped in a quilt whose lover tells her she is beautiful. He tells you that you do not have to try so hard; you are sexy just as you are. He loves the red shirt, the sparkling champagne, and the perfect chocolates. He loves having you to read to. He reads his poems without his glasses, lying naked beside you. He does not like very few foods. His memories of childhood rich and deep, yellow butterfly yo-yos, spring snow.

The day grows cold and cloudy again. The sun cannot sustain itself. Soon it will be too cold to sit on this porch. Even this writing threatens to clam up when you start to prod it too hard.

That's just the point: the journey, not the arrival. Nobody ends up in a safe place with money in the bank and the perfect, loving executor. Everyone dies alone. Think of Charlotte Salomon. She knew as she prepared herself for death in Auschwitz, that the love transcended death.

This moment under the blanket arrests time. There are more forms of arrest than the Nazis imagined. If you keep up this writing, you will have nothing to fear. No fears to gather in the dust-buster like lint and cookie crumbs.

This weather is changing. You in your red halter blurting out radiant truths.

Bestowal

I hold a seashell to my ear
and hear your voice
reading to me
of the sustenance of love
sealed in an envelope.

Something to carry with us
into other hours
when we are alone at a table
and a dog barks.

Love Among the Pencils

A bunch of coloured pencils stood flaring and pointing heavenward in a silver cup. Like lovers, they sang on a summer's night.

One pencil pointed his yellow stem, reached for a pink water-lily floating in a Monet Bay, and then crossed out Monet because maybe it was too literary and escaping the text. He just wanted to transcend the cup. He liked his role as tallest, skinniest pencil and liked to conduct the whole orchestra of coloured instruments whenever his mistress chose to play. She was out dining with friends, but she was sure to return any minute, so the pencil didn't dare blow even the most imaginary kiss at the red passion pen.

This pencil once lived in Nabakov's hotel room and loved butterflies. Higher than the pencil stood the empty *Croustilles et Dinettes* in a wine rack shaped like a bicycle.

"This room needs far more Feng Shui," the mistress said when she appeared with her feather duster. "And besides, it makes me sneeze."

A modern Afghani woman in a low-cut dress, she went to fetch a tray bearing small white mints and cardamon tea. They were a traditional gesture of hospitality where she came from.

"I brought you these this afternoon," she said to the one she loved. "I hope they bring you joy."

She opened the window and let in the falling darkness.

Lolita in the Garden

Over time, the petals span out:
Some have fallen from their stems.
Now these orchids try to protect their yellow centres.
Closed blooms fall, tight little packages.
Better to open the vulnerable heart of the body.

Lolita in pink glasses, just this side of naughty.
She blossoms under the sprinkler, her clothes transparent.

Sea Turtles

After lovemaking, I make the coffee. The conversation rambles deep into the forest of books and people. Feet up, music off or on, shirt off or on, socks lost or found. Bramble of books, records, inspired packages, half-drunk bottles of wine, ashes from a single weed.

We kiss underwater.

At the wall of mourning, our longing brings us close to the tears in things. We know that it all swims away.

I want to say little sideways words that make you write great poems.

The deep lament of your sea turtles is the Om at the end of the day, the oceanic Om of a girl at sea. Your words break the vast emptiness of the evening.

Paging Leonard Cohen

Leonard, where are you tonight?
I e-mailed your manager on Mt. Baldy,
and she appeared in Montreal several years later
sparkling like California wine –
the bird on the wire thrums tonight
with all of the other sweet ones in the garden,
the heavy sun setting in the pink memories of clouds.
A blip in the pattern,
a crack in porcelain letting in light.

Song

*Let everything that has breath
praise the Lord, Halleluya.*
Psalm 150

Praise Him with our dancing feet,
our arms lifting heavy weights
and our hearts rising to greet
what is good in our lives,
what is still painful –
the lover always departing
in Matisse's painting,
her head held in her hand
every morning,
her notebook open.

Praise Him in the old stones
on the cobblestone path
in the large stadium
full of singers and guitars.

Praise Him in the crowded café
where a blonde strokes her hair
as a big song
pours through in a language
you don't understand
but whose feeling is clear –

Praise Him in the stillness
which descends if I continue to etch these black words
onto these blue lines.

The Horse

You can load up a horse with all of the burdens of your life. Feel the pulse in the horse's neck. Bring your breathing into alignment with energy. Load him with your work, your spouse, your child.

My lover flew onto the back of that horse. As light as a feather, he skipped and hopped himself onto that load along with my work, my child. A few friends were heavy, but they made it aboard.

Leonard was the heaviest load of all. I couldn't lift him, actually. I had to leave him behind. He was cumbersome, large. I'm shocked to record this. What can I mean? I was relieved to find how light my lover was, how easily I packed him. Is this because I see him frequently, because of the ethereal connection?

Is Leonard a burden I plan to shed? Do I not need the ballast he provides, the way I eat the porridge he makes with such tender affection – the way he always lets me read the front section of the paper first? Always, I long to dream – to depart on wings unknown. But how much trouble this upward tilt has given me.

"There's too much air in your poetry. You've suffered too much for this passion of yours," said Madeline Dean sternly. A grey-haired earthy woman, she made me cry.

That just turned out to be a hiatus. Will he leave me again? So torn. He thinks he would like to have two families. One to take care of the way he took care of his mother all those years ago, the way he takes care of his wife, placates her in her rages and depressions. One to gaze at the river with in silent contemplation of joy, ducks, water.

Dark, dark, dark. Dark as your beautiful Florida tan, dark as your face holding my hand pressed to your lips for what feels like hours, the intensity of your thoughts filling the room with silence, with uncertainty. All of this time during which you hold my hand thus, I pray. I say one Shema after the other.

"We are in God's hands," I tell him later. Hiding from myself, from him, how shattering his departures are, how heavy the burdens for this horse.

Hotmail

Messages imbed themselves in the roses of evening.
Hot ink scratches over the surface of intelligence.

Eyes fall on the innocent page rough with question marks.
Stopped time crystallizes in fall leaves burning always.

This deep wounding, this dark cut in the side of my soul.
My prayer has roots, sprouts eyes, dresses in carnival clothes.

I write without stopping wearing nothing but my pearls.
Who am I without dance?

I turn off the capitals to turn off my mind.
Love, too, is a confusing thread.

I lost my wildness on the way up Bathurst Street.

In Paris, the women let their bellies show in their tight clothes,
they are beautiful.

The green trees are dark.
Where are you?

I bind my wrist.
Joints ache from passionate playing on the instrument of life.

Found Poem

I start the class on "The Muse's Tragedy."
"Does anyone know what a Muse figure is?"
Rafaelesque Annie in the front row opens her waif eyes.

"Is that like a face that launches a perfume?"

Writing Like a Man

I am wearing my husband's trousers, tie, shirt jacket. My hair pulled severely off my face. Lying on my bed, I sit at my small childhood desk. I no longer have to be two people at once. I, too, can be rock. You portrayed me in your writing as a man, and my muse tells me that tonight I shall sit erect. My Oxford shoes flat on the floor, my pink toenails hidden. No need for a bra. I hoist my elbows onto the desk.

I have cleared the dance memorabilia from the shelf. Curiously, even the small, fat Buddha, male as he is, seems a vestige of my female self. How my right arm tires. My limbs are still my own, whether they are male or female. I thought I would keep the door of the study open, show my true self rather than hide away. The door keeps out the noise.

I write straight up and down. I smell the manly scents of the suit. You look extremely masculine these days. Clean-shaven, some grey. I love what you do to my words.

You've had your run already. You watch your baseball game and occupy your male space. You pin me to a tree, my body moving like the branches, my back like bark.

As a man, can I write from the heart like Mallarmé? I want my cigar, my watch, and my cufflinks. You say you would only wear lipstick if you were going into battle.

My tweed trousers begin to itch. You are curious about my clothes. I like the way you swing my purple money pouch to the side. I must wear new clothes for you. How would you find me tonight, all decked out in Leonard's clothes? The tweed itches at the back of my neck. It is a hot night. I am not Humbert; I am not Lolita. Still, my arm tires. The table is not sound. If I were truly a man, would I worry about the effect of my words?

If I were wearing your clothes, how would I feel? Daddy, Daddy, after dinner smell of cigars and trains. Washroom smells. Old Spice. Talcum powder.

I would bring lilacs in.

This afternoon, I couldn't pee, no matter how I leaned against the tree or how you waved your arms to imitate the sea, the succulent 'S' of the sea. Who'll play *Wall for Pyramus* and *Thisby?*

Be Ocean while I pee. Straddle-legged, filled with champagne, I cannot stand as you do and send my stream down to the earth. You once watched me, and I watched you. Women on pedestals don't pee; Beatrice never does for Dante. It doesn't happen in the lyrical mode.

The Sliver

I close my eyes when you remove the sliver,
allowing you to work in pure concentration.
I open my eyes to watch yours
gazing intently on their task with kavana –
that prayerful mindfulness
you bring to your poems.

Intensity, attention –
what we seek, what we find
in each other's company.
Married to the moment
when we are together,
alive to its possibilities.

Skin Vision

My skin bursts into eyes.

I see below the surface of my life
to what is festering,
brought into consciousness
the way a sauna
makes a blackhead leap out.

Places of infection, disaffection:
secrets kept, blistering feet in hot, tight shoes.

My skin sees what my bones deny:
effort required to make the moments dance.

Soak Your Foot, and Make a Poem Out of It!

I like writing with this cheap pen right now.
It glides along swiftly and does not make a fuss.

Sometimes, correction hurts
like Oxfords too tight for our feet.

Constructive surgery is stilt walking
and constructive criticism may
mould us into a perfect shape we abhor.

You ask me if I am watching videos all week
while my toe heals,
but I've taken a toe-hold on poetry,
upside-down the whole time.

Soon, I'll be running around
with an armful of fresh poems,
cut from these grassy notebooks,
their long stems absorbing water
like my toes in their bath.

Leaving

The women in this generation are packing up the basement
while a June wind howls around the house
as if justice could be found,
as if this dull packing,
each shoe falling,
each box heavier than the last,
were any way to clean out a life
and start anew.

Packing

The evening spreads out wet and wild, my great green coat flapping as I schlep the garbage out for recycling because, somewhere out there in the damp night, he rides his slick car with his warm headlights beaming. He has written hard and furious over the dark night. Over the dark centuries, the people will decide whether we ride the galaxy of immortality. Meanwhile, we have rainy music, jazzy nights.

My father laughs because, on a big steamship, you can forget about all of your problems. You cannot do a thing about them when you are on a short vacation in the middle of the sea by Istanbul.

All of my friends sit around a roaring fire at the foot of a mountain and send negativity packing like old papers settling on shelves, old pens too dry to write. Pack up all your fears in big green garbage bags, the way S— packed up her ambivalence when she left her marriage.

Arrangements

Cars on rain-slick streets:
young men's voices plan out the night
as a bird puts its kids to sleep.

My son's swift steps on the basement stair –
his groan stubby as his beard –
the clink and clank of his arrangements.

Birds speak their own minds,
don't worry what the neighbours will think.
Their fine chirps stir in the darkening sky.

I stop to listen.

And you? Are you out tonight, sparing me the joy you experience
in other rooms?

Birds of a Feather

We two birds bearing books in our beaks,
prayers in our palms,
take flight from mundane matters –

clasp ideas in hours bared for making love –
nest quietly in coloured quilts.

Blue World

What are you thinking
as you gaze at the blue world?
Your shoulders dark,
your coat heavy.

You sit alone
in your basement,
stir a perfect storm
in your jar of words.

A Love Story – A Sheaf

I see you at your desk beneath the picture of Franz Kafka,
your head bent over your notebook writing a love story.
Finding the words. You look up for a moment, and there I
am, carrying a sheaf of my poems – holding them out to
you like rose petals in waxed paper, pressed into memory.

Sunflower ink,
a mustard splash from Irving Layton,
intense as a skunk.

Strong words and thoughts,
truth squirting out from the pen –
they have invented purple ketchup now
because everyone is in love with wizards.

Openness like a summer sky,
a girl's breast
to her lover's hand,
their eyes gazing at one another.

The girl lies on her tummy
reading from Hafiz.
The sudden joy of a butterfly,
white fluttering of wings
above a doily-like wildflower.

Silence

Down into the silence
where his arms
try to shield me
down into the emptiness
of sleep like a heavy burden.

You were out yesterday, and didn't call.
I can't expect you to.
I drew a new, thick line
for you to jump across.
I know that you will approach that line,
peer over its edge.
I may hear from you from the cardboard box
I dreamt you into.
Your voice will squeak.

One day, I looked over at him.
He removed himself from me,
no longer extended tired arms
to comfort me.
Suddenly, I saw him in perfection –
unmasked in blue pajamas –
face soft, untouched, whole.

This morning, I let him hold me.

I face the inevitable,
a bird crashing into a window.

Still, in the garden, there is singing
as I rise, longing only for sleep.

Sacred Space

I

I sit by the water and lean my bicycle against a tree.
Three birds fly by.
I shall write them down in Brautigan's notebook.

We lie on the bed,
      loose pages of your manuscript
surrounding our nakedness
the blankets which unfold us
like the place on your chest I can curl into
while you read,
      pencilling out a word or two on my body
to make it hum.

II
Are you writing today as the cold sun
casts light on brown ground?

letters in a licorice container,
cabinets filled with prose,

silent writing partners
the only correspondent the page.

Sabbath Longing

Poem takes my hand, leads me to my tree,
midnight blue this morning.
I love its colours
when you open the door.
The sun bathes the tree in light;
brown leaves tremble with joy.

I would want you waiting for me,
valentine unwrapped.
As night falls, sadness with it.
Darkening sky brings your absence.
Candles welcome the Sabbath Queen,
words lighting a path to where you are.

Five Silences

The silence of satisfied lovers fills the room,
thick comforters on cold nights,
tympanis on rainy roofs.

The silence of nothing to say,
Stiff, frozen sheets
drying in the cold.

The silence of understood separation –
language suppressed
out of some bitter knowing.

The silence of the mist over these hills,
sweet with the sparrows,
congruent with the wind in the garden.

At home, the couch opens up in the forest
to display the people relaxing on
wicker chairs, eating dinner by candlelight.

The silence of the writer intent on her work.

Post-Surgery

Waking from anaesthetic,
I call for a brass-tack man, who loves me,
but the cavern in my groin, abdominal rip-up,
is the pain you left
when you tore yourself from me –

my bladder, fused to my uterus, ripped a little –
the way my heart tore
when you stood to leave.

Crime

It's a crime
to closet yourself –
yet sometimes,
the trauma is too great,
and it's good
not to be.

Clutter

Clutter everywhere –
files billowing.
The unkempt mind
cannot rest,
needs to be turned out
like a light.

Illness is a form of paralysis.

My old poems
reflect a dead self,
yet I do not know
how to bring this new self
into being.
Raucous music from above.

Nothing seems like a poem –
strangled prose emerges
from a dry throat.

Under Construction

I have raised the set-point of my happiness.

I work on myself like a lumberjack
hammering nails into a little winter cabin,
the teapot for one
boiling gaily.

I watch the light change in the window.
Take care of my wounds.

Eclipse

We're out there on a dark summer night
lying on a baseball field,
looking up at the big black
skullcap of the earth.

Aurora borealis:
a flood of light, a flash of sun.
Big Dipper, Little Dipper,
shooting stars
in the ballgame of space.
God at bat.

Acknowledgements

I would like to thank Merle Nudelman, Jacqueline Borowick, Jay Brodbar, Susan Helwig, and Karen Shenfeld for close early readings of these poems. I would like to give special thanks to Elana Wolff who encouraged me and helped me shape these poems into a collection. I am grateful to my caring, sensitive and nurturing editor, Antonio D'Alfonso for making this book possible.

I would like to express my appreciation to the following anthologies and journals that published some of the poems in this collection: *Cherish Our Heritage* (London, ON: HMS Press, 2004); *Larger Than Life* (Windsor, ON: Black Moss Press, 2002); *Body Language: A Head-to-Toe Anthology* (Windsor, ON: Black Moss Press, 2003); *Hammered Out; Call Online Magazine; Parchment; Surface and Symbol; The Canadian Jewish News; The Writing Space; Lichen;* and *Write Away*.

Born in Hamilton, Ontario, Malca Litovitz is the author of *To Light, To Water* (Toronto: Lugus, 1998; Spanish translation, Alexis Cabrera, 1999) and *At the Moonbean Café* (Guernica, 2003). She was the winner of the 2002 Canadian Jewish Book Award for *To Light, To Water*. A launch for the Spanish translation of this book took place in Havana, Cuba in March 1999. Malca wrote her M.A. thesis on the novels of E.M. Forster while holding the prestigious Dalley Fellowship at McMaster University. She taught English at Seneca College and was a frequent contributor to journals such as *Descant, Parchment, Queen's Quarterly, ARC,* and *Prairie Fire*. Her work is included in eight anthologies and was featured at Harbourfront in 2001. Author of the poetic ballet text, "People Like Us," she was a finalist in the CBC/Saturday Night Literary Competition (1995) and in the Milton Acorn Prize for Poetry (1999). She appeared on radio and television both in Toronto and Havana and spoke on TVO's "Imprint" discussing erotic poetry. In May 2002, she participated in the Hamilton Jewish Literary Festival. In the summer of 2004, her poem "Rain" was featured on 800 buses, streetcars, and subways in Toronto's "Poetry on the Way" series. Malca Litovitz passed away in July 2005.